FAKE

Dennis Balk

Nancy Burson

David Cabrera

Laurel Chiten and Cheryl Qamar

Clegg & Guttmann

Mark Dion and Jason Simon

Duvet Brothers

Tim Ebner

John Glascock

Gorilla Tapes

Day Gleeson/Dennis Thomas

Fariba Hajamadi

Reginald Hudlin

Joan Jubela and Stanton Davis

Annette Lemieux

MICA-TV

Paul McMahon

Branda Miller

Peter Nagy

David Robbins

John Scarlett-Davis

Andres Serrano

Shelly Silver

Michael Smith

Sarah Tuft

With contributions by

Lynne Tillman

Phil Mariani

and an essay by

William Olander

**THE NEW MUSEUM
OF CONTEMPORARY ART, NEW YORK**

FAKE

MAY 7, 1987–

JULY 12, 1987

Library of Congress Catalogue Card Number: 87-42689
Copyright©1987 The New Museum of Contemporary Art
Copyright©1987 Lynne Tillman
All Rights Reserved
ISBN 0-915557-58-4

This exhibition has been made possible in part by grants from the Institute of Museum Services, a federal agency, the New York State Council on the Arts, and the New York City Department of Cultural Affairs.

The individual views expressed in the exhibitions and publications are not necessarily those of the Museum.

This publication has been organized by Phil Mariani, Publications Coordinator, designed by Icon Design, typeset by EyeType, and printed by Conrad Gleber Printing and Publishing.

Cover: Clegg & Guttmann, *An American Family: A Rejected Commission*, 1987.
Photo: the artists.

Frontispiece: Annette Lemieux, *Courting Death*, 1987.
Photo: Cash/Newhouse.

PREFACE

One of the most important issues raised in recent years has been the value of originality. In the visual arts, the original, as a modernist prototype, has been a mark of authenticity and value, inextricably bound up with the artist's hand or signature. Of course, as critics have been quick to point out in recent years, an original is only known (or recognized as such) by virtue of its copies; moreover, many media—among them film, video, and photography—are inherently multiple, problematizing the concept. In a postmodernist world, which appropriates images in order to critique them, the notion of the value of the "original" is losing its tenuous hold.

As concepts of a unified audience, a universal standard of quality, a fixed personal or cultural identity, or a single valid "interpretation" of a work of art are being replaced by a flexible and shifting terrain of ideas and values, artists have begun to use ambiguous forms, recycled styles, "stolen" images, and overt mimicry to confound and rupture the authority of modernist ideology.

The New Museum encourages discourse around these kinds of issues as a means of prompting further investigation and analysis. Thus, questions of authenticity and simulation in the visual arts reflect the ways in which our culture at large has created and is affected by the Age of Simulacra.

My thanks to William Olander, Curator. He has pursued these and other lines of inquiry for several years, and put them into exhibition practice. Thanks also to Phil Mariani and Lynne Tillman for their "original" contributions to the catalogue. We extend our gratitude to the Institute of Museum Services, a federal agency, the New York State Council on the Arts, and the New York City Department of Cultural Affairs for supporting this and similar inquiries into newly-charted critical territory; to our Board, staff, and volunteers for the patience, fortitude, and intelligence they bring to bear on the Museum's behalf; and above all to the artists, for upsetting, once again, the applecart(s).

MARCIA TUCKER
Director

ACKNOWLEDGMENTS

Although the idea for this exhibition dates back to the summer of 1984, the show itself was organized in an extraordinarily short period of time, thanks to the following individuals and organizations: Merrill Aldighieri and Joe Tripican, Robert Beck, Black Filmmaker Foundation, Marcy Brafman, Susan Britton, Christine Burgin, Caesar Video, Tricia Collins and Richard Milazzo, Arturo Cubacub, Electronic Arts Intermix, John Glascock, Jay Gorney, International with Monument, Marsha Kleinman, Carole Anne Klonarides, Marvin and Alice Kosmin, Richard Kuhlenschmidt, Valorie Lee, Annette Lemieux, David Lieber, Paul McMahon, Branda Miller, Maureen Nappi, Jason Simon and Mark Dion, Holly Solomon, Randy Sosin, Lisa Spellman, Miriam Stewart and the Fogg Art Museum, Sarah Tuft, Oliver Wasow and Karen Sylvester, Thea Westreich, and Jamie Wolff.

At The New Museum, many people assisted, as always, in numerous ways: Marcia Tucker, Lynn Gumpert, and Phil Mariani each made useful editorial comments on my essay; Alice Yang did much of the initial research on "real" fakes and coordinated many of the photographs; Russell Ferguson provided the necessary books and catalogues; Karen Fiss, Portland McCormick, Jill Newmark, Cindy Smith, Terrie Sultan, and Jim Minden coordinated all of the production details which make an exhibition happen; and Zoë Brotman and April Garston of Icon Design designed the catalogue with the skill and imagination of seasoned professionals.

I am especially grateful to Phil Mariani and Lynne Tillman for their important and timely contributions to this catalogue; to Christopher Cox, for editing my manuscript; and to each of the artists, not merely for their generosity and cooperation but for their willingness to participate in a project called *FAKE*.

WILLIAM OLANDER
Curator

FAKE
A MEDITATION ON AUTHENTICITY

BY

WILLIAM

OLANDER

—

Elmyr de Hory, Matisse forgery, 1950s, ink on paper, 15 3/4 × 20 1/2 ". Photo: Fogg Art Museum, 1955.54.

To utter the word "fake"; to point a finger and say "fraud"; to declare what was believed to be original, "counterfeit," can promote an extraordinary rupture in the social fabric. To create a fake; to perpetrate a fraud; to pass a counterfeit is literally illegal, but in a broader, metaphoric sense, each constitutes a subversive act which, if not prosecutable, is not easily tolerated. Yet, in a global economy increasingly dominated by high technology capable of reproducing copies more "real" than the real thing, the fake is revealed only with great difficulty. Indeed, for a fake to operate as a fake, it must pass as an original, circulating freely in our system of late capitalism, from the art forgery to the knock-off high fashion, from the pirated record album to the copyright infringement. The question then becomes not necessarily how to identify a fake but how to get rid of one—what happens to the forgery once it is unmasked? Does the sale of a group of fakes, say, by the infamous Elmyr de Hory *as* fakes guarantee that they will not recirculate once again as originals in the near or distant future? The fake is enormously slippery—a strange commodity which, though possessing no value once it is revealed, retains another kind of life precisely because of its newly-acquired "authenticity" as a forgery. It becomes a curiously auratic object, existing in a nether world of otherness. In 1984, for example, three paintings by Piet Mondrian were declared fake by a French court. Michel Seuphor, who originally authenticated the paintings, refused to accept the judgment, stating:

The three paintings have something about them no forger could achieve. Still, supposing the forger were one day identified, I would bow to the evidence. But if today, merely for commodity's sake, I were to admit that the paintings are fakes, and if, ten years hence, other voices were to make themselves heard asserting that they are authentic, what would I look like then?[1]

A long list could be compiled of other recent legal actions concerning fakes and forgeries. In the art world alone, the situation has escalated so dramatically (the amount of money invested in so-called originals has grown so large and indiscriminate) that, according to a recent article, litigations concerning art and legislation intended to regulate it are growing at a rapid and confusing rate.[2]

The discourse on counterfeits, of course, travels well beyond the "real" thing, so to speak, and in the practice of contemporary theory (as opposed to modern philosophy), it

intersects with the discourse on originals. A small group of art historians and critics has addressed this issue in detail and with varying attention to diverse forms of aesthetic production. Rosalind Krauss, for instance, in her continuing investigation into the nature of photography, notes that the most common judgment with regard to a photograph is not about value but about identity—a potentially endless list of possible subjects resulting in confusion and discomfort, not unlike that prompted by the fake, of what a photo is and how it is constituted.[3] Though it is a commonplace in the history of modernism that the activities of the avant-garde have initiated, on the part of the middle-class public which they were intended to shock, a similarly confused response, if not an accusation of "fake," it appears that with the onset of postmodernism, this type of reaction has become more frequent and more subtle precisely because artists have engaged directly with issues, if not of forgeries, at least of copies and reproductions—the art of appropriation, substitutes for the "real" thing. Thus critic Hal Foster, though resisting the temptation to cry fraud, is content to characterize the recent work of Jeff Koons and Haim Steinbach as "'cute commodity' art," which plays "the high-low ambivalence of the readymade . . . right into the ground."[4] The popular press has been less reasonable, quick to use the language of inauthenticity to condemn a new generation as *arrivistes* and opportunists:

> . . . the Neoists fill a gap caused by the excess of demand and the insufficiency of great art. Nostalgia is their most important product—nostalgia for familiar moments in American art history, which can now be reproduced for collectors . . . Nothing about the Neoists is unique except their lust for money—the last chance to shock the bourgeoisie, by embracing it.[5]

Similar cases can be multiplied: the uproar which initially greeted works such as Richard Prince's rephotographs of advertisements (the luxurious commodities—watches, earrings, cigarette cases); the inability of the market to accommodate works such as James Welling's photographs, not just because they are photos (although this is relevant) but because it is impossible to identify what they are photographs of; the tendency to dismiss the early work of Robert Mapplethorpe on the grounds that it is pornographic or merely stylish and thus fraudulent in the context of fine art; or the claim of certain critics that any art that bears a political dimension, a Black aesthetic, for example, is "propaganda, pure and simple."[6] The reverse can also be true when the work is read as "genuine" yet is intended to operate in a dialectical if not critical relationship to the very concept of genuine—the paintings of Charles Clough and Jack Goldstein, the surrogates of Allan McCollum, or Steve Miller's digitized Rorschachs.

Perhaps it is exactly these types of reactions—the classic modern response inserted in the postmodern context which twists it around and renders it its own fraud, its own empty repetition (it's just too easy to cry "fake")—that has prompted a new generation of artists to address these issues head-on. They recognize that the readymade paradigm is no longer fully operable and have sought new strategies which are less obvious and potentially more complex. Appropriation, for instance, is now only one strategy—if it has not been reduced to a style—among many. The figure of Marcel Duchamp is important not in relation to production but in light of behavior: Rrose Sélavy is in the foreground; the chess player assumes prominence; and the desire to make work which is subversive, in the manner of the *Étant Donnés* rather than *Fountain*, is genuine. Having learned from Duchamp, not to mention Andy Warhol, these artists are quickly leaving behind the lessons of modernism, defining themselves instead entirely in relation to theories of postmodernism—politics, aesthetics, sexuality—and their work in relation to the products of post-

Richard Prince, Untitled, 1979, color photograph, 20 × 24". Photo: 303 Gallery.

Robert Mapplethorpe, "Larry and Robert Kissing," 1979, black and white photograph, 20 × 16". Photo: Robert Miller Gallery.

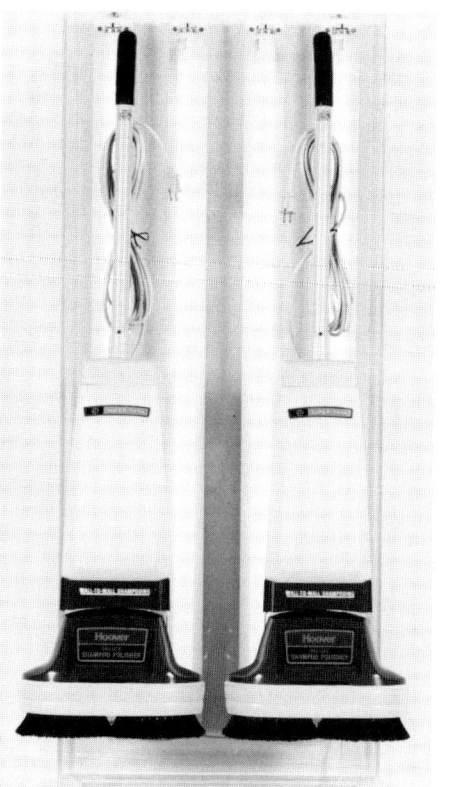

Jeff Koons, "New Hoover Deluxe Shampoo Polishers," 1980, acrylic, fluorescent lights and fixtures, two Hoover shampoo polishers, 56 × 22 × 14". Photo: International with Monument.

modern culture—films, television, recordings, and now the spectacle of art itself: Richard Baim's operatic slide installations, devoted to power and authority, Gretchen Bender's videos, re-presenting the systems of corporate representation; Andrea Fraser's performances, simulating the schizophrenia of institutional discourse; Aimee Rankin's hallucinatory tableaux, fabricating desire, seduction, and consumption. In almost all cases, their work may be seen as proceeding in the fashion not of the true but of the false; in the manner of the "nonhierarchical" described by Gilles Deleuze:

... a condensation of coexistences, a simultaneity of events. It is the triumph of the false claimant.

He simulates father, claimant, fiancé, in a superimposition of masks. But the false claimant cannot be said to be false in relation to a supposedly true model, any more than simulation can be termed an appearance, an illusion. Simulation is the phantasm itself, that is, the effect of the operations of the simulacrum as machinery, Dionysiac machine. It is a matter of the false as power ... [7]

Rosalind Krauss once wrote of a photograph by Sherrie Levine after Edward Weston that it opened backwards, "from behind to the series of models ... of which it itself is the reproduction."[8] This opening backwards has always seemed to be one of the key moments of postmodernism. Modern

Sherrie Levine, "After Walker Evans," 1981, black and white photograph, 8 × 10". Photo: Mary Boone Gallery.

From CHINUA ACHEBE, Girls at War

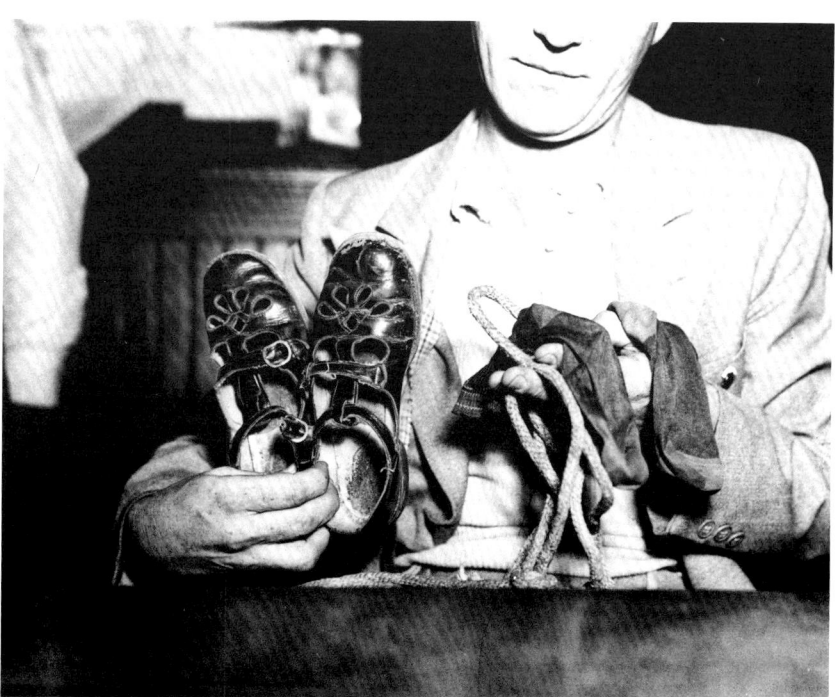

"
That was the day he finally believed there might be something in this talk about revolution. He had seen plenty of girls and women marching and demonstrating before now. But somehow he had never been able to give it much thought. He didn't doubt that the girls and the women took themselves seriously; they obviously did. But so did the little kids who marched up and down the streets at the time drilling with sticks and wearing their mothers' soup bowls for steel helmets .

. . . But after that encounter at the Awka check-point he simply could not sneer at the girls again, nor at the talk of revolution, for he had seen it in action in that young woman whose devotion had simply and without self-righteousness convicted him of gross levity. What were her words? We are doing the work you asked us to do. She wasn't going to make an exception even for one who once did her a favour. He was sure she would have searched her own father just as rigorously. **"**

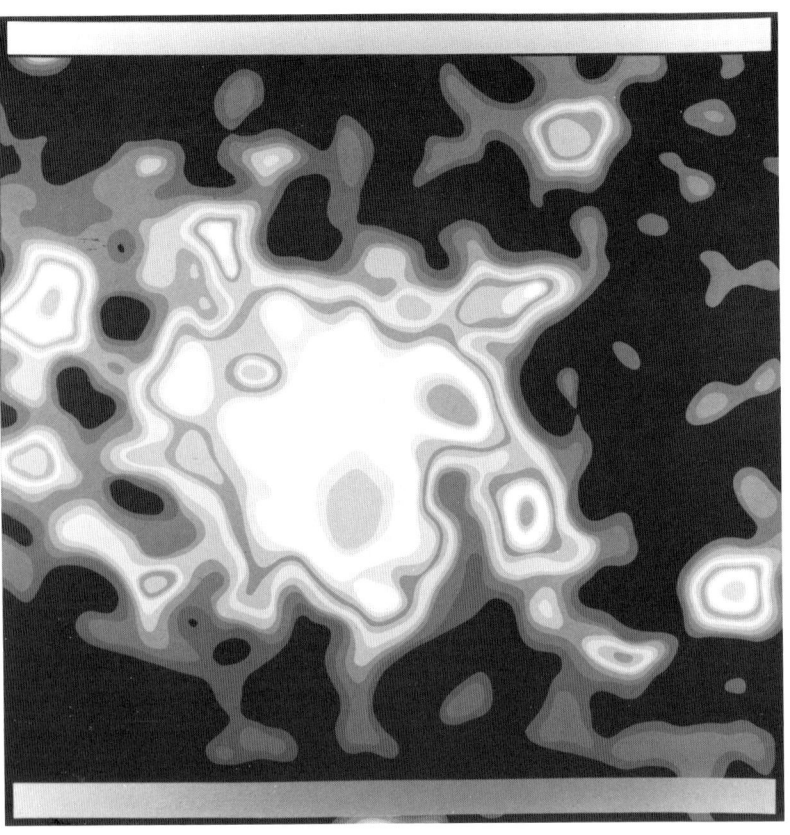

Jack Goldstein, Untitled, 1986, acrylic and metallics on canvas, 72 × 72 × 8 ". Photo: Pelka/Noble.

David Cabrera, "Polystripe #2," 1986. Photo: the artist.

works of art, in contrast, are supposed to function as mirrors or windows, pointing to something "out there" or "in here." They are intended to open outward or inward but not backward; one is supposed to gain insights rather than descend deeper into Plato's cave.

Postmodern works of art, however, like Levine's photographs or her more recent paintings, do not reveal themselves easily; their surfaces are neither transparent nor reflective but densely opaque. Like fakes, they appear to be something they are not and, like counterfeits, they attempt to insinuate themselves quietly into the smooth flow of culture. For example, in this exhibition, works by David Cabrera, Tim Ebner, Fariba Hajamadi, and Peter Nagy proceed in the manner of high modernist paintings. Constructed in like fashion, they are presented in an appropriately artful mode (framed, exhibited singly, in pairs, as diptychs, or in series) and displayed with little explanation. For all practical purposes, they are paintings. Yet, they are also signs of paintings, reified or emptied out, in the current critical jargon, or deconstructed, subverted, and critiqued.[9] But there is also a third option, that they are fakes inserted into the flattened out landscape of all modernist paintings and the institutionalized discourse which demands continuity out of the recent past and seeks to domesticate the radical gesture. These paintings (Cabrera's striped polyester fabric, Ebner's sprayed and poured industrials, Hajamadi's photographs enhanced onto canvas, and Nagy's flat acrylic diagrams) are in fact substitutes. Though "genuine" in their unyielding, nonsensuous, unspectacular, and mechanical character, they refuse to behave as paintings should.

Now let's move a bit further backwards, a few more steps into the cave, where the act of creation begins to become more problematized than in these already problematic paintings, and the identity of the producer loses as much focus as the production. Here, we encounter the incompatible lessons of Pop and Conceptual art colliding with a feminist critique of mastery and a Marxist/Freudian reading of political economy. If this is not immediately apparent in art, it is certainly visible in the spectacle of consumption: what we consume is distinguished neither by its content, form, nor even its sign value, but only by exchange. One thing just as easily substitutes for another and what does this signify but simply more of the same?

The same—*yet different*. This is one of the primary characteristics of postmodernism, displayed, for instance, in the works of Candace Hill, Jenny Holzer, Barbara Kruger, Cindy Sherman, and Laurie Simmons (the constantly shifting nature of the constructed self or a self constructed for you). What makes such difference possible is the understanding that nothing, including art, is fixed; that there are no rules governing the nature of production or production itself; and that "drifting" as a concept and a practice is a natural state. The poststructuralism of the French theorists, such as Jean-François Lyotard, intersects with a feminist discourse on sexuality and

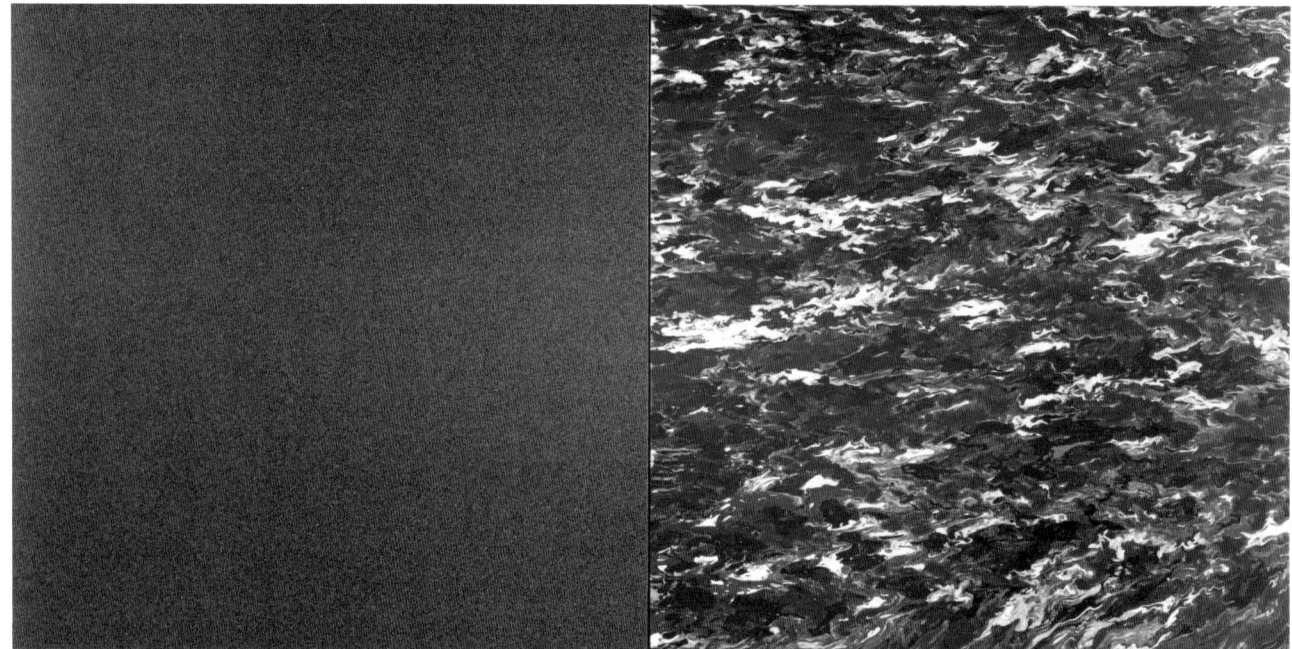

gender, which is equally resistant to claims either to itself or to certainty, celebrating instead the crackup, the fragment, the question rather than the answer. Jacqueline Rose, for example, on Freud:

For Freud, with an emphasis that has been picked up and extended in the work of the French psychoanalyst Jacques Lacan, our sexual identities as male or female, our confidence in language as true or false, and our security in the image we judge as perfect or flawed are fantasies . . . Hence one of the chief drives of an art which today addresses the presence of the sexual in representation—to expose the fixed nature of sexual identity as fantasy and, in the same gesture, to trouble, breakup, or rupture the visual field before our eyes.[10]

This is not to say that the artists participating here seek to engage sexuality *per se* in representation. Rather, theories of poststructuralism, Marxism, and feminism have informed their production and their modes of production, as well as their own awareness of themselves as producers of works of art and aesthetic ideology. Indeed, one of the distinguishing features of much of this work is precisely its lack of an overt criticality.

The art on display in this exhibition is not critical in the received notion of critique, for the latter, like its companion piece, the political, has become so debased, vulgarized, so academic, that it possesses little moral depth or intellectual credibility. (Only the ideologues, a Donald Kuspit, or the more significant community-spirited collectives—Group Material, Tim Rollins & K.O.S.—continue to pursue the critical function, believing either in the market-free analysis or the efficacy of political action.) How is one to maintain some criticality when we reside so exclusively on the inside? A new generation is deeply suspicious of art posing as critique (indeed, of posing itself; as Clegg & Guttmann note: "The idea of pose has been a constant preoccupation. But we don't have a theory of pose, rather our assumption is that by the late twentieth century it's impossible to invent new poses . . .") and has adopted a very different strategy, not unlike that articulated by Thomas Lawson nearly a decade ago:

Better then the . . . spy, the infiltrator, the undercover agent who can make himself acceptable to society while all the while representing disorder. Master of the double bluff, he is able to infiltrate the centers of power in order to undermine the structure from within. An art of representation, a flirtation with misrepresentation. An ambiguous art which

Tim Ebner, Untitled, 1987.

Photo: James Franklin.

seems to flatter the situation which supports it while undermining it. Sweetly arbitrary, art which appears attractively irrational, but which turns out to be coldly rational; art which looks distant, but is deeply felt.[11]

The spy, like the fake, becomes a double agent, infiltrating, subverting, being on the inside and the outside, simultaneously creating and controlling the situation. This is the moment when a new generation watches as the machinery spins its wheels in its always circular desire for the new. And they wait, conscious that any given moment is pure fiction. David Robbins speaks for himself but also for his contemporaries:

Above all, we are reasonable, and consequently are suspicious of artistic practices that promote the neo-divinity of artists. The star search mechanism of the art world is unusable because if we've learned anything from a lifetime steeped in the public fictions of television, movies, magazines, and advertising, it's that people become stars so that their public image may better jump through the hoop of commerce. And for them to jump, someone else must be holding the hoop.[12]

One way not to be dependent exclusively on jumping through the hoop is to produce work that is nonspecific, or not easily identifiable, so that one does not become one's production—a David Salle, a Robert Longo.

Or to produce the reverse: work which rethinks the notion of site-specificity in relation to the much scaled-down economic, political, ideological, and aesthetic arena of the 1980s, an era of dramatically reduced expectations, when the site is again the gallery, but expanded and redefined as a commercial, public, private, or corporate space; Louise Lawler's project of photographing art in situ has become a model of this kind of practice.

Artists such as Mark Dion and Jason Simon, Annette Lemieux, and David Robbins are exemplary in their refusal to specialize. Others, like Dennis Balk, John Glascock, Day Gleeson and Dennis Thomas, Paul McMahon, and Michael Smith, simply choose not to (Smith has developed his entire career on a single identity, "Mike," while his production has been heterogenously unpredictable to the extreme). Thus, on one occasion, Annette Lemieux may exhibit a high modernist abstraction similar in appearance *and* feeling to the late works of Ad Reinhardt, which is engaged with the discourses both on copies and originals and on the end of painting (it was Reinhardt, after all, who claimed that he was "just making the last paintings which anyone can make"). On another, there is no painting in sight but rather a collection of books haphazardly arranged on an Alpine-

Fariba Hajamadi, "The Hearing of Deaf Actions, the Seeing of Blind Thoughts," 1987. Photo: Ellen Wilson.

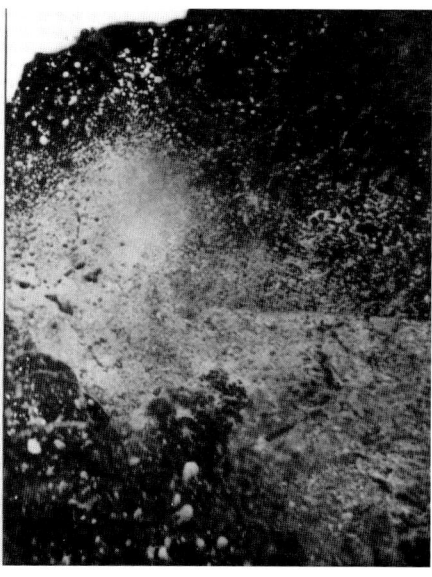

style shelf, setting up and off a chain of reactions. Is it a response to the commodity sculpture of her male contemporaries; more significantly, an indication that her project is not to be defined exclusively (or at all) by the medium of painting and is, in fact, highly conceptual in origin; or a provocative illustration of the collision between high culture and kitsch, no longer to be seen as the battleground that critics have characterized it but an open field from which to break down false distinctions, constructed hierarchies, and male-defined systems of aesthetic ideology. Though nothing about Lemieux's work can be simply tagged "feminist," by "eluding definition" it "calls attention to the way feminism participates in a larger and more encompassing direction, the investigation of cul-

Peter Nagy, "Econo-Crash," 1986. Photo: the artist.

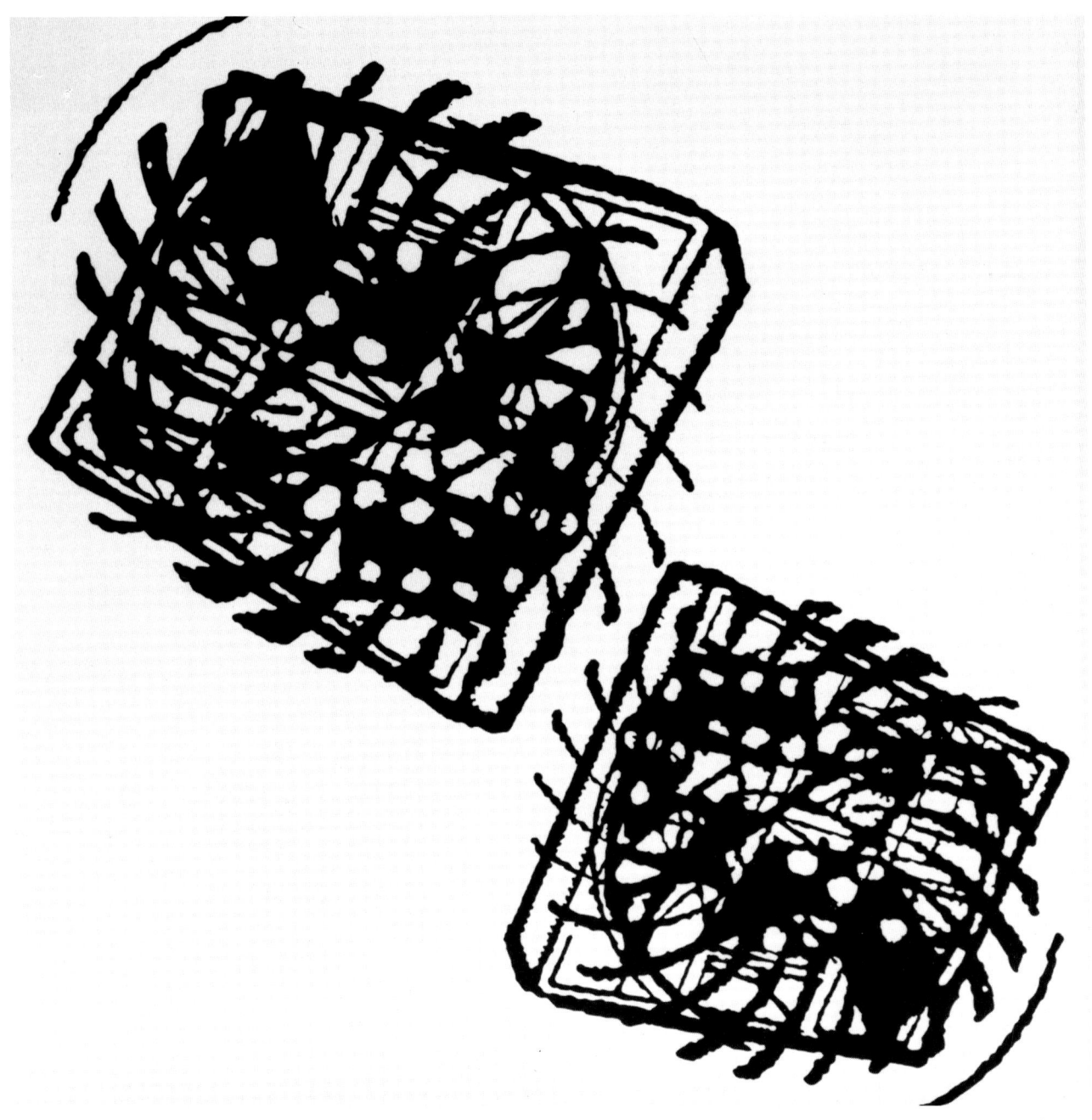

From J.M. COETZEE, "The Narrative of Jacobus Coetzee," in Dusklands

" Most frontiersmen have had experience of Bushman girls. They can be said to spoil one for one's own kind. Dutch girls carry an aura of property with them. They are first of all property themselves: they bring not only so many pounds of white flesh but also so many morgen of land and so many head of cattle and so many servants, and then an army of fathers and mothers and brothers and sisters. You lose your freedom. By connecting yourself to the girl you connect yourself into a system of property relationships. Whereas a wild Bushman girl is tied into nothing, literally nothing. She may be alive but she is as good as dead. She has seen you kill the men who represented power to her, she has seen them shot down like dogs. You have become Power itself now and she nothing, a rag you wipe yourself on and throw away. She is completely disposable. She is something for nothing, free. She can kick and scream but she knows she is lost. That is the freedom she offers, the freedom of the abandoned. She has no attachments, not even the wellknown attachment to life . . . . "

Cindy Sherman, "Untitled Film Still," 1978, black and white photograph, 10 × 8". Photo: Metro Pictures.

Barbara Kruger, Untitled, 1981, black and white photograph, 60 × 40". Photo: Mary Boone Gallery.

tural constraints."[13]

From a different direction, David Robbins assumes a similar strategy, by producing work which possesses no center, dedicated as it is to slippage, displacement, rupture, and erasure. As a photographer, for instance, he has produced photographs that teeter on the edge of the found and the forgotten, the discarded. One series is devoted to slogan-buttons all using the word "Fuck," pinned to the likes of a Ralph Lauren polo shirt ("Fuckin' A"). Another is comprised of glamorous, commercial-looking abstractions that possess the look of art but are strictly accidents of artifice and the camera. And a third is a collection of portraits of eighteen young "emerging artists," in the parlance of the museum or gallery, headshots that transform them into actors and actresses taken not by himself but by a theatrical photographer. As Peter Nagy, one of the subjects, quipped three years ago: "Due to massive hype and exposure, the art world is on the verge of becoming something it's never been before. More in the vein of popular culture, movies, television, fashion. It's competing for that segment of *Newsweek* magazine, that four-page color spread." Distance operates to full effect in Robbins's work, informed, as it is, by a fair amount of cynicism, a constant undermining of the elevated and the self-important—an attitude that is still repugnant to many, even the most cynical, in the so-called community of art and artists. Belief in the transcendent does not die easily and in an age of inauthenticity, sincerity is still an amazingly marketable quality. Robbins has developed an artistic persona that is like an irritant, and his work seems to exist in order to provoke a negative reaction.

Let's introduce two more actors onto the stage, or into our cave, a third modus ope-

randi, and a third type of production. Mark Dion and Jason Simon's current work-in-progress, a thirty-minute film tentatively titled *The Art of History*, began as an exhibition by Dion in 1985. At the same time, Simon produced a similar investigation into real estate—a short film on the redevelopment of Times Square. Dion's project consisted of three "original" eighteenth- or nineteenth-century paintings and three texts briefly describing the transformation of each one from something it was to something it was not. For instance, *Economic Recovery*, a genre "painting," is discovered to be a reproductive print glued to a canvas and then repainted. Rather than restoring the object to its original condition as a print, a conservator cuts it down and reworks it so it will again pass as a painting. The project was subsequently published in *Real Life* magazine (Summer 1985) under the title "Tales from the Dark Side," which allowed a closer reading: "The print that was a painting, then a print, is once again a painting (although quite a bit smaller). The painting is framed and sold. The original COLLECTOR, the AUCTION HOUSE, the RESTORER, and the DEALER have all made a good deal of money off a nineteenth century scam."

Louise Lawler, "Arranged by Louise Lawler," 1982, installation at Metro Pictures, New York. Photo: Metro Pictures.

The "painting," of course, reappears in Dion and Simon's film, as does the "tale," the entire project now simulated as a commercial documentary. Indeed, what began as a rather modest project, bearing some resemblance to both Hans Haacke's investigations (for instance, *Seurat's "Les Poseuses"*) and Louise Lawler's "displays," has been developed into its own "forgery," so to speak, devoted to the point at which the restorer's art becomes indistinguishable from the forger's, and the fake indistinguishable from an original, circulating freely in the market thanks to its *restoration*. Obviously, our meditation on authenticity is becoming more complicated, and what has been implied thus far as a "politic" is becoming clearer, even as we are pushed, almost unaware, further over to the "Dark Side." For the investigation into art restoration leads not merely to the constructed systems of representation which constitute the "aesthetic" but equally to the ideological state apparatuses which support them: the institutions which continue in their nineteenth-century affiliations—the museum, university, auction house, gallery—as well as in their updated versions—the corporation, foundation, and advisory firm. It is but a short step from this project to other, equally "political" productions, such as Day Gleeson and Dennis Thomas's "restoration"—a modest attempt to "correct" a corporate takeover of a well-known print by Rembrandt—or, one step further, Dennis Balk's "simulations"—works resembling the forms of advertising (posters, book and magazine covers, kiosks) but which specifically advertise ideology rather than product.

In an ironic twist, the film of Mark Dion and Jason Simon, in its approximation (or appropriation) of a popular form—the educational documentary—begins to lead away from the discourse on high culture to which, inevitably, paintings lend themselves (paintings are still the construct upon which most of the art apparatus rests) and toward

Annette Lemieux, "Sonnet," 1987, books, wood, and paper, 50 × 33 × 5 1/2 ". Photo: Cash/Newhouse.

the arena of popular, or mass, culture—an area greatly expanded since the 1930s when Clement Greenberg, for instance, first articulated the antagonistic relationship between what he called the "avant-garde and kitsch." For Greenberg, the latter—everything from magazine illustration to academic realism, from ceramic figurines to photographs—*determined* the former, i.e., the presence of kitsch propelled the avant-garde to create ever more distinct and autonomous forms of art which could not be confused with kitsch, the manifestation of working-class culture.[14] Rigid distinctions were made and maintained between the two, as well as equally rigid distinctions between the audience for one (elite, upper-class, intellectually or economically, preferably both) and that for the other (lower- to middle-class white and blue collar workers), as well as the site—the museum versus the movie theater, for example. Though certain developments associated with the avant-garde incorporated elements of kitsch (especially Dada and Surrealism), it was only when the two became indistinguishable from each other *in the same work* did, in the recent re-reading of Thomas Crow, "the privileged moments of modernist negation occur . . . when the two aesthetic orders, the high and the low, [were] forced into scandalous identity." Crow cites as an illustration Georges Seurat's monumental postimpressionist painting *Sunday Afternoon on the Island of the Grande Jatte*.[15]

In postmodernism, something quite different occurs—the terms are reversed. That is, for modernism the confusion between high and low operates primarily on the level of content; the "switching of codes" to which Crow refers is basically iconographic, taking place more often than not, even in the disruptions prompted by cubist collage, in the privileged site of the oil painting. In postmodern practice, the reverse is true (consequently, the most important precedents for postmodern production are not the received achievements of modernist painting but the accomplishments of the Russian avant-garde, Dada, and Surrealism). In other words, for postmodern-

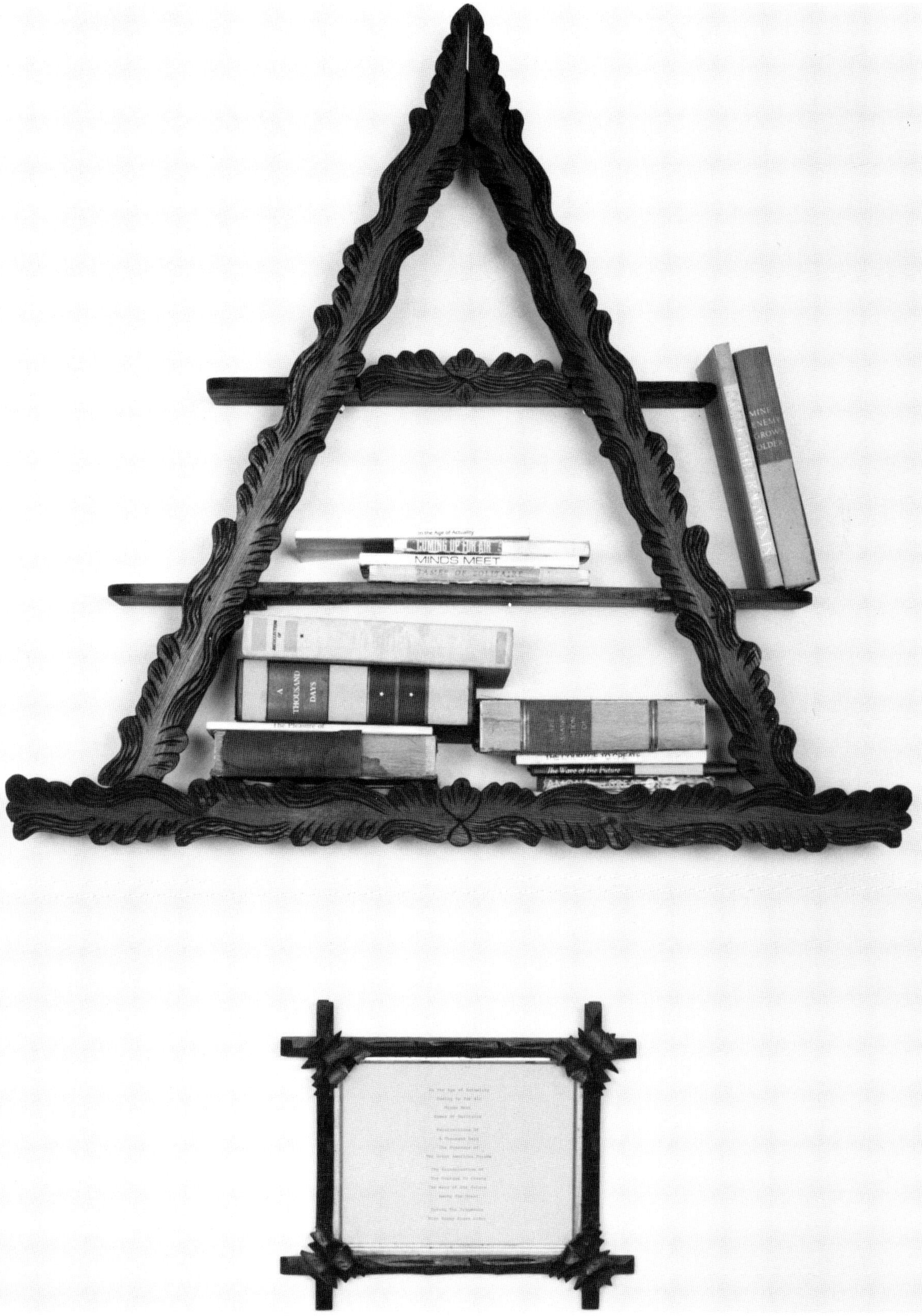
MINE ENEMY GROWS OLDER
In the Age of Actuality
COMING UP FOR AIR
MINDS MEET
GAMES OF SOLITAIRE
A THOUSAND DAYS
The Ware of the Future

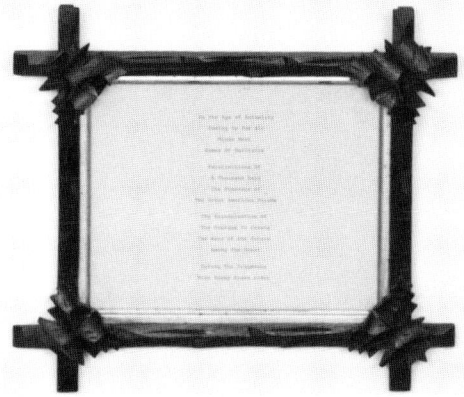

From RICHARD CONDON,
Winter Kills

" ... We were prepared to go on weaving scenarios until we had exhausted you. Fictionalized facts. Fantasized facts. Those are the steady cultural nourishment of the American people, forcefed down their throats through the power hoses of the most powerful and pervasive overcommunications design ever dreamed of by man to enslave other men. Still, the sublety of lying can be fun, as we all know. It wasn't the exposure of the Watergate tragedy that told Americans of the glorious Freedom of Their Press Institutions—also called the Triumph of the Little Man Over the Forces of Repression—because, after all, the Glorious Free Press and the readers of that press had known about the Watergate since June of 1972, well before the presidential elections, in time for the Glorious Free Press to expose the Forces of Repression and prevent them from ever reaching the White House again. The skill there was that we could experience the thrill of the fantasy of a free press through which the Watergate was re-exposed, after our free press had gotten permission to do so. And that is where our collective genius really lies—in the extraordinary American ability to perceive only when we are told to perceive and to believe only when we are told to believe. Not before. "

Peter Nagy

Mark Dion and Jason Simon, "Artful History, A Restoration Comedy" (production still), 1987. Photo: Moyra Davey.

ism the "switching of codes" is operating primarily in terms of form, while issues of content are more specifically focused on "difference." Indeed, the most important instances of postmodernism are those activities that appropriate the forms of popular culture, *without* necessarily appropriating its contents, so the artwork itself is no longer dependent exclusively on the totalizing site of high culture (the museum) and other audiences may be genuinely addressed (the same audiences that voraciously consume magazines, billboards, television, records, and films). What Greenberg could not predict in 1939, and what he and his apologists have resisted ever since, is that certain forms assumed by kitsch would become, beginning in the 1950s, the most significant forms of almost any culture—high, low, official, sub-, or in-between: rock 'n' roll transformed into postminimalism, reggae, punk, and new wave; motion pictures turned into film; television made into video; and theater manifested as performance. Indeed, what are we to make of a situation where nearly identical works can function both within the arenas of art and of commerce?

For example, *Melos* is the title of a photograph produced in 1985 by Clegg & Guttmann in their manner; that is, as an uncommissioned group portrait of four well-dressed white males who, in their "real lives," are specialists in chamber music known as the Melos Quartett. This over-scale work of art was then used, with the permission of the photographers, as the cover photo for Deutsche Grammophon's record album, *The Melos*

David Robbins, "Talent (Peter Nagy)," 1986, black and white photograph, 10 × 8 ". Photo: the artist.

Hans Haacke, "Seurat's 'Les Poseuses' (small version), 1888-1975," 1975 (detail), ink on paper (printed), 30 × 20 ". Photo: John Weber Gallery. (page 28)

WHITTAKER CHAMBERS,
affidavit given to the FBI

" Sometime in either 1933 or 1934, I met a young fellow on the street in New York. I was footloose and fancy-free. Well, I took him to a hotel—I don't remember where it was—just some hotel. That night I had my first homosexual experience. It was a revelation to me. Because it had been repressed so long, it was more violent than it would otherwise have been. It set off a chain reaction in me which was almost impossible to control. Since that time, continuing up to the year 1938, I engaged in numerous homosexual activities, both in New York and Washington. I actively sought out opportunities for homosexual relationships; these took place in Minneapolis, Pennsylvania, and Washington D.C. In 1938, I managed to break myself from my homosexual tendencies. This does not mean that I was immune to such stimuli, only that my self-control was complete, and I thereafter led a blameless life as husband and father. The Hiss forces, of course, will seek to prove that my weakness entered into my relations with Alger Hiss and possibly others. This is completely untrue. Having testified mercilessly against others, it has become my function to testify mercilessly against myself. This is not from love of self-destruction, but because only if we are consciously prepared to destroy ourselves in the struggle can the thing we are fighting be destroyed. "

"Les Poseuses"
(small version)
purchased 1922 for $5,500 by

John Quinn

Born 1870 Tiffin, Ohio. Son of Irish immigrants. Father James William Quinn, prosperous baker in Fostoria, Ohio. Mother Mary Quinlan, orphan. Sister Julia married to William V. Anderson, successful pharmacist of Fostoria. Sister Clara nun of Ursuline Convent, Tiffin.

Graduate of Fostoria High School. 1888 at University of Michigan. 1890-93 in Washington, D.C., as private secretary of Secretary of the Treasury Charles Foster (friend of Quinn family), under President Benjamin Harrison. Graduates from Georgetown University Law School 1893, Harvard University Law School 1895.

1893 clerkship in New York law firm of General Benjamin F. Tracy. 1900 junior partner with Alexander & Colby. 1906 own law practice specializing in financial and corporate law. Offices at 31 Nassau Street in Wall Street district.

Chief Counsel to National Bank of Commerce, second largest bank in U.S. Instrumental in acquisition of Equitable Life Assurance Society by Thomas Ryan, financier with extensive interests in coal, tobacco, Congolese and Angolan diamond mining. His chief counsel as of 1906. Negotiates merger of Bowling Green Trust and Madison Trust with Equitable Trust, 1908-1909. New York Stock Exchange counsel on tax law, 1913. Special counsel to N.Y. State Comptroller in inheritance tax proceedings against estate of John Jacob Astor, 1914. Represents munitions makers in Federal Tax case, 1917. Submits brief in Congress for adoption of Alien Property Act, same year. Represents U.S. Alien Property Custodian and private American interests in suit over seizure of German properties. Wins 1920 in U.S. Supreme Court establishing the law's constitutionality (legal fee $174,000).

Tammany Hall Democrat. Delegate to National Convention 1908 and 1912. Campaigns for candidacy of Oscar W. Underwood against Woodrow Wilson. Theodore Roosevelt a personal friend.

Staunch supporter of Irish causes. Contemptuous of American cultural life, francophile, anti-semitic, anti-German; proposes to French President Poincare take-over of German Ruhr industries by Allies, 1923.

Collects 19th and 20th century French and English painting and sculpture, including Cézanne, van Gogh, Gauguin, Seurat, Derain, Matisse, Picasso, Duchamp-Villon, Brancusi, Epstein. Investment in art estimated at $500,000. Has personal contact with artists in Paris and London. Helps with organization and promotion of Armory Show, 1913. Conducts successful campaign in Congress for the exemption of modern art from customs duty. Wins in Congress tax exemption of art sales by living artists, 1918.

Sponsors U.S. tours of Irish writers and theater productions. Assists in the publication of works by W. B. Yeats, J. M. Synge, Joseph Conrad, T. S. Eliot, James Joyce. Extensive correspondence with writers. Buys literary manuscripts, including all of Joseph Conrad's. Sells most in auction 1923 (Conrad for $110,000 and Joyce's "Ulysses" for $2,000). Defends "Ulysses" against obscenity charges in New York Court.

Lives, as of 1911, in top floor apartment at 58 Central Park West. Frequent travels to Ireland, England, and France. Remains bachelor, though has several romances.

Member of numerous exclusive clubs, of Contemporary Art Society, and Société de Cent Bibliophiles. 1915 appointed Honorary Fellow of Metropolitan Museum, 1918 Chevalier of Legion of Honor.

Dies of cancer in New York, 1924.

Photo around 1921. From "The Man from New York," by B. L. Reid

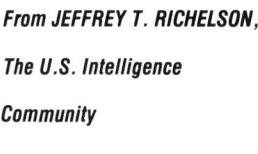

From JEFFREY T. RICHELSON, *The U.S. Intelligence Community*

" Strictly speaking, intelligence activities involve solely the collection and analysis of information and its transformation into intelligence, but several other activities have come to be considered examples of intelligence activity—specifically, counterintelligence and covert action....

Covert action can be defined as any operation or activity designed to influence foreign governments, persons, or events in support of the sponsoring government's foreign policy objectives while keeping the sponsoring government's support of the operation a secret. Thus, while in the case of clandestine collection the emphasis is still on keeping the activity secret, the emphasis in covert action is on keeping the sponsorship secret.

There are several distinct types of covert action: black propaganda (propaganda that purports to emanate from a source other than the true one); gray propaganda (in which true sponsorship is not acknowledged); paramilitary or political actions designed to overthrow or support a regime; support (aid, arms, training) of individuals and organizations (newspapers, labor unions, political parties); economic operations; and disinformation. "

Day Gleeson/Dennis Thomas, "Master Etchers," 1987. Photo: the artists.

"Master Etchers," advertisement, GCA Corporation, 1986.

Quartett. In its turn, the latter was photographed by the artists and is presented here as a third work called *Our Production/The Production of Others.* The question becomes: does each begin to cancel the other out as either art or kitsch and become a third term, like advertising? (As demonstrated, each can so easily become the other.)

Some observers would certainly respond in the affirmative, stating that the avant-garde no longer exists (having exhausted itself or, in its turn, having been co-opted) and in its place, the forms of popular culture have assumed prominence. Some might even call this process a democratization of culture, whereby popular forms replace those of the bourgeois avant-garde. Film, video, and photography replace the commodious easel painting, sculpture, and print. Or is it a matter of displacement rather than substitution or democratization—that slippery moment when art becomes commerce and shifts back again? Or, as the photographs of Andres Serrano suggest, when art becomes a form of popular religious experience or an expression of ethnicity. But perhaps it is more a matter of disequilibrium, a rupture of the conventional orders, hierarchies, and distinctions, that opens a space of desire which is not regulated but placed into constant, self-conscious circulation. That the forms, practices, and contents of popular culture have become the dominant forms of cultural enterprise and expression in the West is neither surprising nor necessarily alarming. Since the 1940s, particularly in the United States and Europe, with the advent of advertising and marketing on a massive scale, artists have turned consistently to mass culture in order to challenge the very issues of uniqueness, originality, autonomy, and self-referentiality upon which the traditional avant-garde rested. This is not to

From J. LAPLANCHE and J.-B. PONTALIS, The Language of Psycho-Analysis

"

Hysteria: Class of neuroses presenting a great diversity of clinical pictures. The two best-isolated forms, from the point of view of symptoms, are conversion hysteria, in which the psychical content is expressed symbolically in somatic symptoms of the most varied kinds: they may be paroxistic (e.g. emotional crises accompanied by theatricality) or more long-lasting (anaesthesias, hysterical paralyses, "lumps in the throat," etc.); and anxiety hysteria, where the anxiety is attached in more or less stable fashion to a specific external object (phobias) . . . . Freud aligned himself with a whole current of opinion which saw hysteria as a "malady of representation." It was of course in the process of bringing the psychical aetiology of hysteria to light that psycho-analysis made its principal discoveries: the unconscious, phantasy, defensive conflict and repression, identification, transference, etc.

"

Dennis Balk, left: "Over the Weekend" (detail), 1987; right: panels from the "Bulletin Series," 1987, duratrans, 24 × 24". Photo: the artist.

deny that much of what has been produced in these areas, from Pop art to the artistic agitprop of our time, has been reabsorbed into renewed discussions of the avant-garde—the new avant-garde, the neo-avant-garde, the post-avant-garde—or into the institutions of high culture themselves (the double bind of fame and money and the co-optive powers of the system are often too much to resist even for the most contrary of art and artists). Today, however, certain mass cultural forms and practices, including film, photography, video, and computer-generated techniques, still stand relatively apart from the dominant forms of Fine Art culture, refusing, in many ways, to be assimilated and, at the same time, being refused, precisely due to their "popular" character, their artifice, their fraudulence, their tendency to be something other than art. Nancy Burson's computer-assisted composite portraits, for example, are just as likely to be found in the pages of *Rolling Stone* or on the nightly news as matted, framed, and hanging on the walls of the museum. As Douglas Crimp noted five years ago in relation to photography:

. . . photography is too multiple, too useful to other discourses, ever to be wholly contained within the traditional definitions of art. Photography will always exceed the institutions of art, always participate in nonart practices, always threaten the insularity of art's discourse.[16]

Works of "video art" (not to mention "computer art") are particularly vexing in this regard, even though this is a relatively recent problematic. Ten years ago, video art was still clearly designed within the field of the avant-garde, i.e., both production and criticism were defined in *opposition to* popular culture or—in David Antin's now classic phrase—to television, video's "frightful parent." Though some alternatives have developed in an equally oppositional relationship to this basically formalist dichotomy, a substantial

Clegg & Guttmann, "Our Production/The Production of Others," 1986. Photo: the artists.

From ALICE Y. KAPLAN,
Reproductions of Banality

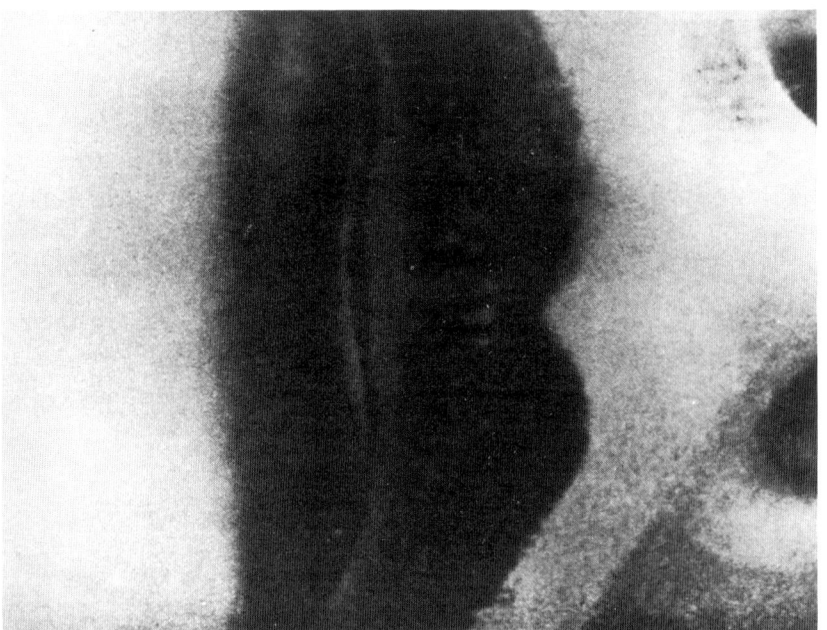

" ... what fascism transforms is not the means of production or distribution of wealth in the state, but the technical means by which the state reproduces its own legitimacy before individuals. When fascism took over, it took charge of the imaginary, using the most advanced sophisticated agents of representation available—cinema, radio, architecture, staged rallies—new elements in the "design" of everyday life that few knew to take seriously as political forces.... Participation in fascism was not as selflessly masochistic as its most outraged, disbelieving critics would have it appear, for it gave the masses the impression of intimacy, not just with the leader, but with the myriad representations of themselves supplied by the state. "

amount of current writing on video still posits the fundamental distinction between the two, a distinction necessary to maintain in order to preserve the "highly personal nature of video art" in contrast to the "lowest common denominator" of broadcast TV.[17] There is, of course, justification in approaching video from the direction of television cautiously. Over thirty years ago, Theodore Adorno noted the ideological effects of television as "a medium of undreamed psychological control. The repetitiveness, the self-sameness, and the ubiquity . . . tend to make for automatized reactions and to weaken the forces of individual resistance."[18] And a new generation of television critics have analyzed it in similar though updated terms, focusing on television's simulations or the economic and political imperatives of broadcast TV.[19] Obviously, the early experiments in video were attempts to avoid the pitfalls of television. But these attempts, more often than not, resided almost exclusively within the institutions of high culture, including public television, and have since become memorialized as masterpieces of video art or transformed into the latest accommodating genre—the museum or gallery "installation."

In the 1970s, however, dissenting voices were occasionally heard which did not simply repeat the rather naive video/television dichotomy or the equally simplistic Fine Arts/Mass Culture rift. Jack Burnham, in 1975, was one of the first (if not the first) to speak of "Television Art," in which the "perennial problem of 'quality' besetting High Art" is not relevant, since video is "more interested in the day-to-day problems of acting effectively in various social contexts."[20] Other critics noted more simply that video had been greatly influenced by television style and genre and one posited, in relation to work produced in Southern California, that television is video's "real subject."[21] Examples invariably included the comedic tapes of William Wegman and the self-consciously parodistic ones of John Baldessari, but also the more metacritical productions of Richard Serra (*Television Delivers People*) and Martha Rosler (*Semiotics of the Kitchen*) and works that were made specifically for broadcast, like Chris Burden's *TV*

Nancy Burson, "Marilyn Monroe Update," 1986, black and white photograph, 8 × 10 ". Photo: the artist.

Andres Serrano, "Gold Christ," 1987. Photo: the artist.

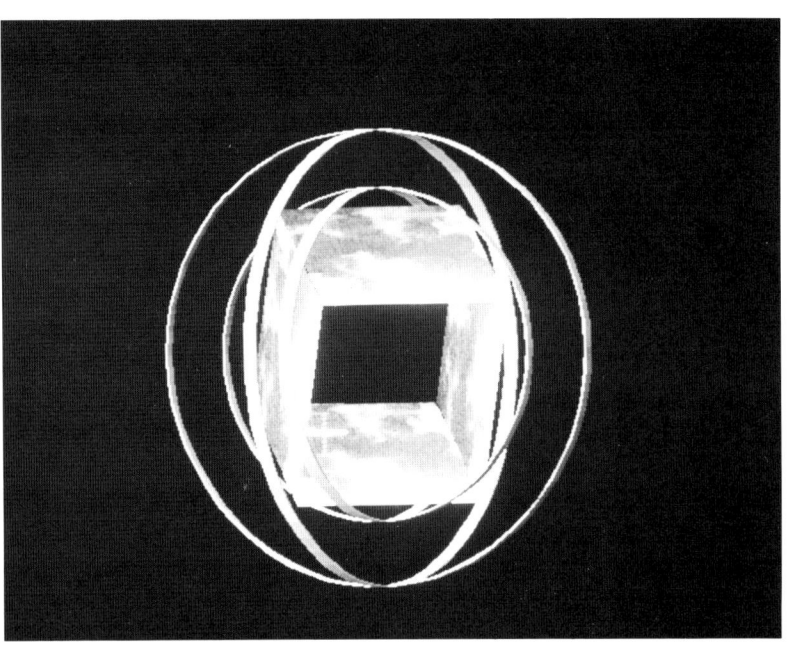

John Glascock, "Enfin," 1987. Photo: the artist.

Branda Miller, "That's It Forget It," 1985. Photo: Marita Sturken/Electronic Arts Intermix.

Whether or not fame and aura have descended on the major figures of "Television Art" is less relevant today than the "kinship" certain works of video share with the standard forms of broadcast TV, to the point at which they are indistinguishable from, not the programs, but television's *raison d'être*, the advertisements. Indeed, one of the works produced for this exhibition—John Glascock's *Fake*—is an ad for the exhibition itself. What distinguishes tapes like Glascock's from previous works of video art is the desire to establish a dialectical relationship to TV, simulating the forms of television without reproducing its contents. Today's video artists are intensely aware that one of the reasons art is carefully delineated from commerce is largely a function of commerce itself. And in order to mount some resistance to the commercialization process, one must engage with and within the field of television, from the guerrilla experiments of the late 1960s and early '70s (TVTV, Antfarm) to the current productions of cable and low power TV (Paper Tiger Television, the Closet Case Show), from the more subversive moments of *Saturday Night Live* to the rare intervention of a work made for the music television network, MTV—the anti-apartheid "Sun City" produced by Steve Van Zandt, or the "Artbreaks" created by, among others, Richard Prince (an American Express commercial), Jean-Michel Basquiat, and Dara Birnbaum.

Though most of what has been produced in the area of "television art" possesses little dialectical function, there are significant exceptions, many of which have been programmed here. Let's note immediately: despite the "look" of television, with one exception none of these tapes was commissioned by the entertainment industry, and the pieces that most closely resemble music videos have no record to sell. Branda Miller's rock video parody, for example, *That's It Forget It*, is an extremely affecting look at the lifestyle of some upper-middle-class Los Angeles teenagers. It was produced in collaboration with Miller by the kids themselves and consequently is a far cry from

Ad, which aired daily in Los Angeles for one month in 1973. As Burnham remarked, "The alternative television movement in part beguiles the art audience by its kinship with the omnipotent powers of network television, so that some of the aura of network programming, with its fame and money, descends on the mundane figures of Television Art."[22]

Joan Jubela and Stanton Davis, "Bombs Aren't Cool!" 1986. Photo: the artists.

most of what is on MTV, which is illustrative, star-dominated, and lifestyle-oriented. (Approximately ninety-six percent of all music videos programmed on television, whether MTV or network, are paid for and provided by the record companies and are predominantly devoted to mainstream, white rock 'n' roll groups.) As Michael Nash has noted, "Radiovision [an obsolete term for television] is a zone where individual videos merge into a seamless continuum of consumer caress and enticement."[23]

Like Miller's "MTV," the tapes by Stanton Davis and Joan Jubela, Paul McMahon, John Scarlett-Davis, and Sarah Tuft, along with the "scratch" videos of the British groups, Gorilla Tapes and the Duvet Brothers, combine found, off-air, and original footage with a musical soundtrack in a rock video mode but unlike anything visible on TV—in each case, a visual satire or intervention which often has the power and humor of a John Heartfield montage.[24] In a different manner, MICA-TV's "commercials" for artists (Laurie Simmons, R.M. Fischer) approximate the forms of commerce perfectly (a "teaser," an "industrial") while still maintaining a fair amount of ironic distance. Michael Smith's *Mike*, produced for the current *Saturday Night Live*, is the perfect fake-out in that the character which Smith has perfected to the point where it acts as his double ("Mike") functions both in the collective psyche formed by television (Ralph Kramden, Beaver Cleaver, Mary Richards) and as an advertisement for himself. Finally, the tape called *Two in Twenty* by a lesbian collaboration headed by Laurel Chiten and Cheryl Qamar, stands as a model work which has appropriated the form and much of the style of the conventional soap opera, while injecting it with an entirely other content. The fact that the work-in-progress (it will run for five hours) is focused exclusively on lesbians, with an occasional hetero or male homosexual, is indicative of the producer's desire to insert difference, conflict, and dislocation into a field normally characterized by homogeneity and resolution. On the other hand, in relation to the standard fare of broadcast soaps, constructed out of a steady diet of murder, incest, and betrayal, *Two in Twenty*'s subject may appear entirely too mundane—too everyday, too banal to be significant when compared to the sensationalized contents of *General Hospital*, *Dallas*, and *Knots Landing*, not to mention of the movie-of-the-week, devoted to child abuse, drug addiction, alcoholism, sexual dys-

Paul McMahon, "Mild Style," 1984. Photo: the artist.

GEORGE ORWELL (1944)

> It is not clear at first glance why hatred of democracy and a tendency to believe in crystal-gazing should go together....
>
> ... the claim that "there is nothing new under the sun" is one of the stock arguments of intelligent reactionaries. Catholic apologists, in particular, use it almost automatically. Everything that you can say or think has been said or thought before.... It is not very difficult to see that this idea is rooted in the fear of progress. If there is nothing new under the sun, if the past in some shape or another always returns, then the future when it comes will be something familiar. At any rate what will never come—since it has never come before—is that hated, dreaded thing, a world of free and equal human beings. Particularly comforting to reactionary thinkers is the idea of a cyclical universe, in which the same chain of events happens over and over again. In such a universe every seeming advance towards democracy simply means that the coming age of tyranny and privilege is a bit nearer. This belief, obviously superstitious though it is, is widely held nowadays, and is common among Fascists and near-Fascists.
>
> In fact, there are new ideas.... Ideas may not change, but emphasis shifts constantly. It could be claimed, for example, that the most important part of Marx's theory is contained in the saying: "Where your treasure is, there will your heart be also." But before Marx developed it, what force had that saying had? Who had paid any attention to it? Who had inferred from it—what it certainly implies—that laws, religions, and moral codes are all a superstructure built over existing property relations? It was Christ, according to the Gospel, who uttered the text, but it was Marx who brought it to life. And ever since he did so the motives of politicians, priests, judges, moralists and millionaires have been under the deepest suspicion—which, of course, is why they hate him so much.

function, AIDS, political corruption, toxic waste, and nuclear annihilation—all topics that the television industry somehow expects the global public to accept as "real." It is, of course, precisely this double-edged relationship to both television and video art that dramatically distinguishes *Two in Twenty*, as well as Reginald Hudlin's satirical variety-show look at American television and race relations in *Reggie's World of Soul*, and Shelly Silver's *Meet the People*, a fifteen-minute "documentary" devoted to lifestyles of the upwardly mobile.

What is significant about so many of the works present in *FAKE* is the recognition by their producers that television specif-

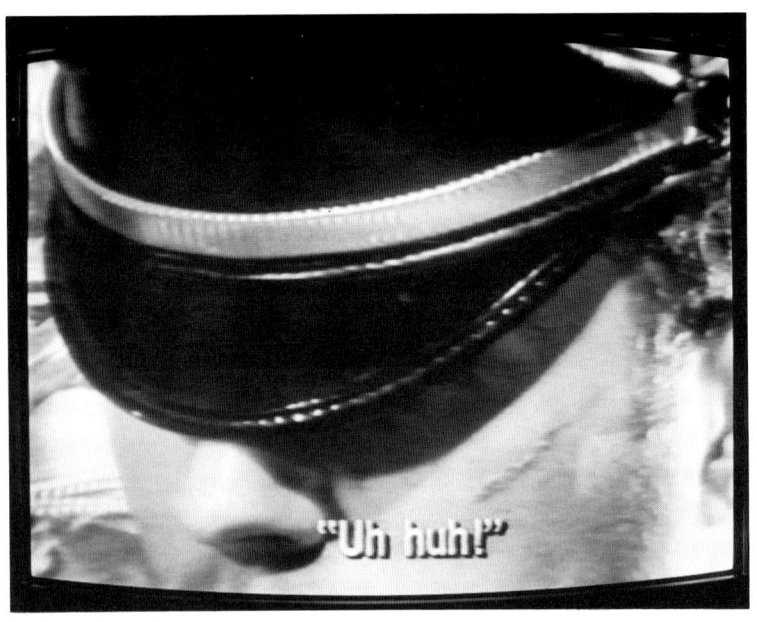

ically, and mass culture in general (but increasingly that which is generated from the sphere of computer and electronic technosciences), does *not*, number one, constitute a tradition in any modernist fashion; number two, that in its nontradition, there is nothing, in modernist fashion, to rebel against; and number three, by not positing a rebellion *against*, artists can mount an exploration *of*, which, in Lyotard's formulation, "leads to experimentation, which is poles apart from experience."[25] Experimentation is what *FAKE* is about—a modest attempt, hardly on the scale one would like (see Lyotard's museological project, *Les Immateriaux*), to undermine the humanist project which continues to promote a totalizing spirit of creativity, traversing all perceptible forms to arrive at a complete expression of self ("an aesthetics grounded on the 'absolute' genre of the speculative narrative, on the form of finality, and on metaphysical arrogance").[26] On the contrary, *FAKE* promotes a new practice that weaves its way through a multiplicity and incommensurability of works, from signs of paintings to simulations, from artifice to artificial intelligence, from the present to the distant future. *FAKE* asks the question, "What do we want of art today?" and frames it against the forgery and the counterfeit, thereby interrogating the original and recognizing that such a dichotomy is wholly modern. And surely, one thing that we can be certain of is that to be modern is not what we want of art today.

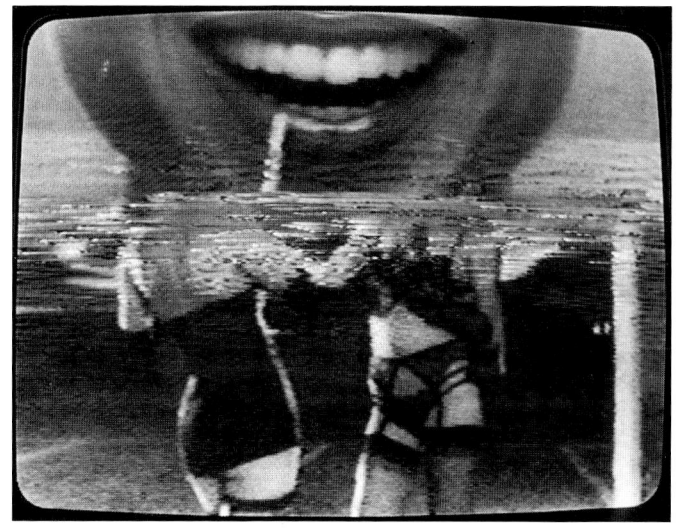

Sarah Tuft, "Don't Make Me Up," 1986. Photo: the artist.

John Scarlett-Davis, "A Trip Through the Wardrobes of the Mind," 1983. Photo: Marita Sturken/Electronic Arts Intermix. (above left)

Gorilla Tapes, "Secret Love," from "Death Valley Days," 1984. Photo: Marita Sturken/Electronic Arts Intermix. (below left)

The Duvet Brothers, "Blue Monday," 1984. Photo: Marita Sturken/Electronic Arts Intermix.

Notes

1. Quoted in Michael Gibson, "For the Love of Mondrian," *Art News* 84, no. 8 (October 1985): 122. Similar claims were made by Jean Decoen in the 1940s for the genuineness of one of the most famous twentieth-century forgeries, Vermeer's *The Disciples at Emmaus* by Han Van Meegeren; see Denis Dutton, ed., *The Forger's Art* (Berkeley: University of California Press, 1983), pp. 45, 61. The opposite, however, is more likely to be the case. For example, when a Grunewald acquired by the Cleveland Museum of Art in 1977 was subsequently discovered to be a forgery, then-director Sherman E. Lee, who purchased the picture, claimed that it "fell to pieces" before his eyes. Cited in Joseph Alsop, "The Faker's Art," *New York Review of Books* 33 (October 23, 1986): 30.

A rather different discussion concerning fakes has recently emerged with regard to the security of originals. An article by Donald Brook in the British journal *Art Monthly*, responding to a theft from the National Gallery of Victoria (Melbourne), suggested that museums, rather than improving security, might better exhibit fakes, or "scrupulously exact facsimiles." Like most writers, however (see note 3), Brook provocatively asks this question only to ask the other: "Couldn't it be that at a moderate distance in ordinary light, and even though you can't *tell* the difference, there *is* a difference [between the copy and the original]?" Donald Brook, "Art and Authenticity," *Art Monthly*, no. 99 (September 1986): 2.

MICA-TV, "R.M. Fischer: An Industrial," 1983.

Photo: the artists.

A related project has been proposed recently to the New Museum: an exhibition, "The Museum of Museums," produced by an Italian firm, of one hundred masterpieces from Giotto to Warhol, "doubled . . . replicas of the highest quality, yet unique works, the perfection of which rivals that of history's great forgeries . . . " Curiously, the project duplicates that of artist Elaine Sturtevant, who has been producing to-scale copies of twentieth-century masterworks since the mid-1960s.

2. Sophie Burnham, "As the Stakes in the Art World Rise, So Do Laws and Lawsuits," *New York Times*, February 15, 1987, Section 2, pp. 1, 28.

3. Rosalind Krauss, "A Note on Photography and the Simulacral," *October*, no. 31 (Winter 1984): 58. This work should be seen in opposition to, for example, the works cited in note 1 which, despite their raising the issue of "whether authenticity truly matters in the visual arts" (Alsop, p. 29), always respond in the affirmative. Krauss, on the other hand, seeks to problematize the question rather than resolve it. See Rosalind Krauss, *The Originality of the Avant-Garde and Other Modernist Myths* (Cambridge, Mass.: MIT Press, 1985).

4. Hal Foster, "(Dis)agreeable Objects," in *Damaged Goods: Desire and the Economy of the Object* (New York: The New Museum of Contemporary Art, 1986), p. 17. Also see by the same author, "The Future of an Illusion, or The Contemporary Artist as Cargo Cultist," in *Endgame: Reference and Simulation in Recent Painting and Sculpture* (Boston: Institute of Contemporary Art, 1986). There, Foster observes of the same work that it is "largely subsumed by sign exchange value—and that *in this logic art works are no different than vacuum cleaners or basketball*

Michael Smith, "Mike," 1978.

Photo: Pelka/Noble.

Laurel Chiten and Cheryl Qamar, "Two in Twenty," 1987. Photo: the artists.

Reginald Hudlin, "Reggie's World of Soul," 1985. Photo: Floyd Weber.

shoes . . ." (pp. 97, 99).

5. Kay Larson, "Masters of Hype," *New York Magazine*, November 10, 1986, p. 102 (a review of work by Meyer Vaisman, Jeff Koons, Peter Halley, and Ashley Bickerton).

6. The quote is Hilton Kramer's; see Tilden J. LeMelle and Margaret G. LeMelle, "Art and Race: Pursuit of a Black Aesthetic," in *Race and Representation* (New York: Hunter College Art Gallery, 1987), p. 26.

7. Gilles Deleuze, "Plato and the Simulacrum," *October*, no. 27 (Winter 1983): 53.

8. Rosalind Krauss, *Originality*, p. 168.

9. See Hal Foster, "Signs Taken For Wonders," *Art in America* 74, no. 6 (June 1986): 80-91, 139. This is not to suggest that the projects of these four artists are identical. Obviously, Nagy's "cancer paintings," as the series is known, comprised of reconstituted pop and corporate emblems, are quite different from Hajamadi's (equally ambiguous) cropped and collaged photographs of "nature" on canvas.

10. Jacqueline Rose, "Sexuality in the Field of Vision," in *Difference: On Representation and Sexuality* (New York: The New Museum of Contemporary Art, 1984), p. 31.

11. Thomas Lawson, "Spies and Watchmen," *Cover* 1 (Spring/Summer 1980): 17.

12. David Robbins, "The Guiding Light," in *Infotainment* (New York: Livet Reichard Co., Inc., 1985), p. 22.

13. Kate Linker, "Eluding Definition," *Artforum* 23, no. 4 (December 1984): 61.

14. Clement Greenberg, "Avant-Garde and Kitsch," in *Art and Culture: Critical Essays* (Boston: Beacon Press, 1961), pp. 3-21. Also see, Thomas Crow, "Modernism and Mass Culture," in *Modernism and Modernity* (Halifax: The Press of the Nova Scotia College of Art and Design, 1983), pp. 215-265.

15. Crow, "Modernism and Mass Culture," pp. 244-245.

16. Douglas Crimp, "Appropriating Appropriation," in *Image Scavengers: Photography* (Philadelphia: Institute of Contemporary Art, 1982), p. 33.

17. Kathy Huffman, "Video Art: A Personal Medium," in *The Second Link: Viewpoints on Video in the Eighties* (Banff: Walter Phillips Art Gallery, 1983), p. 30. For a critique of the institutionalized discourse of video, see Martha Gever, "Pressure Points: Video in the Public Sphere," *Art Journal* 45, no. 3 (Fall 1985): 238-243. Some of the ideas found in the following pages are elaborated in my forthcoming essay, "Video, Television, and Popular Art: On the Work of Bruce and Norman Yonemoto."

18. T. W. Adorno, "Television and the Patterns of Mass Culture," in *Mass Culture*, ed. Bernard Rosenberg and David Manning White (New York: The Free Press, 1957), p. 476.

19. See, for instance, Michael Sorkin, "Faking It," in *Watching Television*, ed. Todd Gitlin (New York: Pantheon, 1986), pp. 162-182, and David James, "inTerVention: the contents of negation for video and its criticism," in *Resolution: A Critique of Video Art*, ed. Patti Podesta (Los Angeles: Los Angeles Contemporary Exhibitions [LACE], 1986), pp. 84-93.

20. Jack Burnham, "Sacrament and Television," in *Video Art* (Philadelphia: Institute of Contemporary Art, 1975), p. 91. "Television art" has become a rallying point for a new generation of video artists and critics such as John Sanborn and Carl Loeffler, the editor of *Art Com* magazine. The latter has been particularly zealous in his claims for "a populist television art" that will reconcile fine art and popular culture; see Loeffler, "Toward a Television Art: Video as Popular Art in the Eighties," in *The Second Link*, pp. 14-20. A criticism of this position is Lucinda Furlong, "Getting High Tech: The 'New' Television," *The Independent* (March 1985): 14-16. A more reasonable view of "artists' television" is expressed by Robin White, "Great Expectations: Artists' TV Guide," *Artforum* 20, no. 10 (June 1982): 40-47.

21. Kim Levin, "Video Art in the TV Landscape," in *New Artists Video: A Critical Anthology*, ed. Gregory Battcock (New York: E. P. Dutton, 1978), p. 67.

22. Burnham, p. 92.

23. Michael Nash, "An Artists' Guide to Music Television," *Art Com* 7 (1984): 12-19. The literature on music television is growing rapidly, and a sampling of conflicting views might include the following: Jody Berland, "Sound, Image, and the Media: Rock and Social Reconstruction," *Parachute* (1985-1986): 12-19; John Wyver, "Television and Postmodernism," in *Postmodernism: ICA Documents 4* (London: Institute of Contemporary Art, 1986), pp. 52-54; Eric Breitbart, "Agit Rock Video: Music TV Goes Political," *Sightlines* (Spring/Summer 1986): 24-26; Bill Brown, "I Want My MTV: Dire Straits' Money For Nothing," *Buffalo Arts Review* 4 (Spring 1986); David Tafler, "The Economics of Renewal: Music Video and the Future of Alternative Filmmaking," *Afterimage* 14, no. 2 (September 1986); and Pat Aufderheide, "The Look of Sound," in *Watching Television*, pp. 111-135.

24. See Jeremy Welsh, "Scratch and the Surface: Contemporary British Video," *Afterimage* 13, no. 6 (January 1986): 4-5.

25. Jean-François Lyotard, "Philosophy and Painting in the Age of their Experimentation," *Camera Obscura* (Summer 1984): 122.

26. Ibid., p. 123.

Shelly Silver, "Meet the People," 1986. Photo: the artist.

MADAME REALISM'S IMITATION OF LIFE

BY LYNNE TILLMAN

A cigarette hung from Madame Realism's lips, invitation to disaster, for with it there she noticed that few people came over to talk to her. Sometimes Madame Realism felt as if she just didn't exist. Maybe it was her imagination, but she put the cigarette out anyway, using the museum's floor because there were no ashtrays. Under the weight of this relatively new stigma, she hummed aloud, "Another opening, another show," and walked past everyone she knew, without looking at the art, heading for the ladies room. How easy it is to become a social outcast, she reflected, which made her want another cigarette as she approached a door with a sign on it. Like many of the bathroom signs around the city, this one proved difficult to read, and as Madame Realism felt that all signs were signs of the time, she wished she could have instantly known whether it was unisex or not, and was relieved to find inside small stuffed chairs and large full-length mirrors, a stage set from some previous time. This must be parody, she thought, sitting on the toilet, notebook in hand, and entered this in a large scrawl: IS PARODY A CONDITION OF AMBIVALENCE, WHERE DISDAIN AND NOSTALGIA MIX? AND JUST MIGHT BE THAT CRAZY THING CALLED LOVE? DON'T FORGET TO WRITE ABOUT THE TIME I WENT INTO A BATHROOM AND IT TURNED OUT TO BE SOMEONE'S ARTWORK. ARTIST CAME RUNNING WHEN I FLUSHED TOILET. Madame Realism flushed the toilet and put her notebook away.

Standing in front of a full-length mirror, she was startled to see herself once again. It was always weird to see what she was inside of, her conduit, so to speak. Certainly Madame Realism tried to control her image and hoped to register as someone with a sense of style, even if that style was hers alone. Madame Realism feared seeming au courant in a desperate and hungry way, yet wanted to be of her time, not to deny its marks on her, something not true of persons called mentally ill, their faces and bodies stamped by their troubles, their clothes thrown together, signifying distress. One does not want to seem disturbed even in disturbing times. But who can really control how other people see you? Madame Realism opened her notebook: GUY AT PARTY SAID HE HAD FOUR FAKE TEETH IN FRONT. DOES THAT TURN YOU OFF? HE ASKED. OFF WHAT? I

ANSWERED.

Two women rushed the mirror and smiled at Madame Realism, whose reverie was interrupted as she quickly hid her notebook. "Are you really Madame Realism?" one asked. "Not really," she answered, continuing to smile. "Why, do I look like her?" All three women looked at themselves and each other in the mirror, and Madame Realism made a face she never made unless she was looking at herself in a mirror. Apart from the opposite image problem, Madame Realism silently noted the left side/right side dilemma that everyone faced. Their faces lacked symmetry and it evidenced life's contradictoriness, even its betrayals. Hadn't a friend with a baby recently told her that infants lie, or dissemble, almost from birth, pretending to be in pain when they simply want attention. Lying, Madame Realism's friend said, is obviously necessary for survival.

One of the women said, "This isn't a good mirror," and Madame Realism relaxed a little, the idea of a perfect mirror terrifying anyway, and besides she didn't like the way she looked just then. Still, she thought, if there is no inner life or self, and I'm not being conduited, this physical presence, this facade, might be all one really did have. This raised the image stakes immeasurably, making the peculiarity of her image to herself even more burdensome. On the other hand, it could be consoling to know that that empty feeling is not just a feeling. After Madame Realism left the room, one woman said, "I think that is Madame Realism, but do you think a fictional statement can ever be true?"

Shaking her head from side to side, Madame Realism returned to the large space, so open that its transient inhabitants could lose themselves for a moment or two, and lie like babies. As if they'd never be found out. The test of a good friendship is the ability to keep secrets, she thought, and avoided walking near someone who might tell her one. In this room full of fellow co-conspirators—conspiracy is merely breathing together—suddenly Madame Realism wanted to flee.

Perhaps she'd been in town too long. Never wanting to outlive her welcome, Madame Realism every once and a while disappeared, without telling anyone, and returned some months later, reassured. For as much as she needed to leave, she needed to return. One produced the other, in a sense.

There are ways to leave without leaving, suggested a friend. A cultural sleight of hand might be to dress as a man, to become Sir Realism, for instance. Madame Realism told him she could never be Sir Realism, but that one time

'soviet girl' an american hoax

pat harper cries

she had attempted to dress as a man, for a costume party, and had bought a tuxedo and everything that went with it. But with the outfit on and her hair slicked back with gel the consistency of aspic, she'd transformed herself into just the kind of man she couldn't stand. Or that she'd never be attracted to.

That she could become that which repelled her shocked her in a way that only falling in love over and over again usually did. "I was," she told her friend, "like a quotation from a work or book I hated." Disguise in this instance uncovered more than it covered. "What'd you end up wearing?" the friend asked. Madame Realism said she put on a long black velvet skirt, a black and white checked jacket from the Thirties, and tied a loose, floppy bow around the neck of the tuxedo shirt. She pretended to be a French or English governess from the Thirties. Everyone else was either in bondage outfits or in nineteenth-century gowns. She talked with a book editor whose face was entirely covered by a leather mask, except for his lips. She said she had a great time. Madame Realism's face clouded over. Maybe, she thought, I didn't look like a French governess from the Thirties.

The phrase "life drawing" popped into her mind, almost like a cartoon, and Madame Realism complained to her friend that she had always been bad at it. Her people had been too big for the drawing paper, essential parts like heads or legs left off. Larger than life were they? her friend teased. Yes, like a movie, she smiled. From art imitating life, to life imitating art, and here they were at art imitating art and life imitating life. But instead of Frankensteins and golems running around town, versions of Diane Keaton as Annie Hall. Or that man Madame Realism had seen near the Algonquin, dressed just like James Joyce as recorded by a famous photograph of the author taken in the Twenties. Imitation of life or art or both? Madame Realism sighed audibly. Perhaps imitation is the insincerest form of flattery.

Nothing ever worked the way it was supposed to, everything having unintended effects, and all you could do was get used to it. Like getting used to living in a world of knock-offs, she mused, and said goodbye to her friend, leaving the opening without ever having looked at what was on the walls. If asked she could say she had been temporarily blinded, and truly, as she walked along Broadway, staring in windows but not seeing anything, it was as if her provisional lie might be true. MADAME REALISM REVEALED AS A HOAX, she wrote in her notebook. Just a matter of survival she reassured herself, whose lie would be insignificant compared with Wendy Ann Devin's. For one brief moment, Wendy Ann Devin had been news in the *New York Times*. 'SOVIET GIRL' AN AMERICAN HOAX, the headline read. A certain Valeria Skvortsov, 14, a Soviet hockey player from Kiev, is really Wendy Ann Devin, 21, of Braintree, Massachusetts. Wendy/Valeria convinced residents of Brainerd, Minnesota, and other communities, that she was a well-known Soviet hockey player, whose father was a Soviet pilot. He had left her in the States, she said, to fend for herself. Wendy's real father turns out to be a Braintree, Massachusetts cop, says Sergeant Ball, the detective assigned to the case. Sergeant Ball explains, "Apparently she's got an obsession with hockey," a quote that ends the story. Wendy had

the last one, a young man whose eyes met hers for a brief moment. She turned to watch him ask others, noticing how they, like she, avoided "the homeless" in similar ways. Anything she thought about people who had no homes sounded as canned as a studio audience's laugh track or a recorded announcement over a P.A. The word homeless itself naming, cate-

no taxation without representation

posed as at least five different Soviet hockey stars and had even crossed over to Canada where she got herself a Soviet visa, and in doing so nearly was deported from the U.S. Wendy Ann Devin, where are you now? And, who are you now? Madame Realism wondered. No charges had been filed against her, but she was urged to seek psychiatric help. And what does her disguise reveal? To have portrayed herself as an abandoned and homeless Soviet girl? Perhaps a longing to unstate herself, maybe like the yearnings of would-be transsexuals who find themselves submerged in the wrong body. In Wendy Ann's case, the wrong body politic. Could this be the unconscious' attack on nationalism, that which binds body and psyche to place of birth? A *New York Post* story might have read: WENDY BETRAYS BIRTHRIGHT. NOT SINCE ESAU SOLD HIS BIRTHRIGHT TO JACOB....

Madame Realism walked home, lost in thought, interrupted only by people asking for money. She gave a quarter to

gorizing, and dismissing in one blow. And so unrepresentable were these people, Pat Harper had impersonated one on TV, to get "their" story across, but which became the story of the anchorwoman who cried on television. PAT HARPER CRIES, Madame Realism wrote in her notebook, followed by: IS THE UNREPRESENTED LIFE WORTH LIVING? And, NO TAXATION WITHOUT REPRESENTATION.

Inside her home, the one she could afford to leave and return to, voluntarily, every once in a while, she felt the evening unravel like a badly knit sweater. And soon it would be all gone, like Wendy Ann Devin, who had disappeared into thin air, along with the homeless and the people at the opening. Thin air. Madame Realism walked over to her window and looked up at the dark sky, the kind that in the country would be full of stars. But here just a few were visible, positioned economically, almost like asterisks or reminders. Madame Realism left the next day.

WORKS IN THE EXHIBITION

Height precedes width. Works preceded by an * are illustrated in this catalogue.

DENNIS BALK
Born in 1952. Lives in Los Angeles.

* *Over the Weekend*, 1987
  Formica, duratrans, fluorescent light,
  84 × 23 × 23 ″
  Collection of Randy Sosin, Los Angeles

  On Monday or Tuesday, 1987
  Formica, duratrans, fluorescent light,
  84 × 23 × 23 ″
  Courtesy of the artist

NANCY BURSON
Born in 1948. Lives in New York City.

  Untitled #5, 1985-86
  Cibachrome, 11 × 14 ″

  Untitled #42, 1986
  Cibachrome, 11 × 14 ″

  Untitled #51, 1986
  Cibachrome, 40 × 30 ″

  Reproportioned El Greco, 1986
  Cibachrome, 10 × 8 ″

  Courtesy of Holly Solomon Gallery, New York; software by David Kramlich; the images were filmed on a Celco color recorder, courtesy of Celco

DAVID CABRERA
Born in 1956. Lives in New York City.

* *Polystripes 2, 5, 6, 7, 10*, 1986
  Polyester on birch, each: 60 × 32 ″
  Courtesy of 303 Gallery, New York, and two private collections

LAUREL CHITEN AND CHERYL QAMAR
Born in 1955 and 1950. Live in Sommerville, Massachusetts.

* *Two in Twenty: A Lesbian Soap Opera* (excerpts from a work-in-progress), 1987
  Color video, 12 minutes
  Courtesy of the artists

CLEGG & GUTTMANN
Born in 1957. Live in New York City.

* *Our Production/The Production of Others*, 1986
  Cibachrome, 120 × 120 ″
  Courtesy of Jay Gorney Modern Art, New York

* *An American Family: A Rejected Commission*, 1987
  Cibachrome, 60 × 80 ″
  Courtesy of Cable Gallery, New York

MARK DION AND JASON SIMON
Born in 1961. Live in New York City and San Diego.

* *Artful History, A Restoration Comedy*, 1987
  Installation, with paintings and photographs, dimensions variable
  Courtesy of the artists

THE DUVET BROTHERS
Born in 1956 and 1957. Live in London.

* *Blue Monday*, 1984
  Color video, 4 minutes
  Courtesy of Electronic Arts Intermix, New York, and London Video Arts

TIM EBNER
Born in 1953. Lives in Los Angeles.

* *Untitled*, 1987
  Zolatone and decoglo on canvas, 2 panels, each: 30 × 30 ″
  Courtesy of Kuhlenschmidt-Simon, Los Angeles, and Wolff Gallery, New York

  Untitled, 1987
  Zolatone and decoglo on canvas, 2 panels, each: 30 × 30 ″
  Courtesy of Kuhlenschmidt-Simon, Los Angeles, and Wolff Gallery, New York

JOHN GLASCOCK
Born in 1954. Lives in New York City.

  Fake, 1987
  Color video, 45 seconds

* *Enfin*, 1987
  Color video, 45 seconds
  Courtesy of the artist

DAY GLEESON/DENNIS THOMAS
Born in 1949 and 1955. Live in New York City.

* *Master Etchers*, 1987
  Framed etching, 22 × 27 ″
  Framed by Max Hyder

  Collector Prints, 1986
  Color photograph, mounted, with frames, 60 × 40 ″

  Art for Discriminating Taste, 1986
  Color photograph, mounted, with frame, 20½ × 14 ″
  Courtesy of the artists

GORILLA TAPES
(Joe Dovey, Gavin Hodge, and Tim Morrison)
Live in London.

* *Death Valley Days*, 1984
  Color video, 10 minutes 30 seconds
  Courtesy of Electronic Arts Intermix, New York, and London Video Arts

FARIBA HAJAMADI
Born in 1957. Lives in New York City.

* *The Hearing of Deaf Actions, the Seeing of Blind Thoughts*, 1987
  Photographic emulsion on canvas, 3 panels,

56 × 44 ″ or 56 × 36 ″
Courtesy of Christine Burgin Gallery,
New York

REGINALD HUDLIN
Born in 1961. Lives in New York City.

* *Reggie's World of Soul*, 1985
Color video, 30 minutes
Courtesy of The Black Filmmaker Foundation,
New York

JOAN JUBELA AND STANTON DAVIS
Born in 1955 and 1953. Live in New York City.

* *Bombs Aren't Cool!*, 1986
Color video, 5 minutes
Courtesy of the artists

ANNETTE LEMIEUX.
Born in 1957. Lives in New York City

Vital Organ, 1986
Oil on canvas, 96 × 48 ″
Collection of Thea Westreich, Washington,
D.C.

* *Courting Death*, 1985
Color photograph, 48 × 38 ″
Collection of Marvin and Alice Kosmin,
New York

Walking on Water, 1985
Color photograph, 38 × 24 ″
Collection of Jamie Wolff, New York

PAUL MCMAHON
Born in 1950. Lives in New York City.

* *Mild Style*, 1984
Color video, 3 minutes 18 seconds
Courtesy of the artist

MICA-TV
(Carole Ann Klonarides and Michael Owen)
Born in 1951 and 1952. Live in New York City.

* *R.M. Fisher: An Industrial*, 1983
Color video, 3 minutes 30 seconds
Courtesy of Electronic Arts Intermix, New York

BRANDA MILLER
Born in 1952. Lives in New York City and
Los Angeles.

* *That's It Forget It*, 1985
Color video, 4 minutes 30 seconds
Courtesy of Electronic Arts Intermix, New York

PETER NAGY
Born in 1959. Lives in New York City.

* *Econo-Crash*, 1986
Acrylic on canvas, 72 × 72 ″
Courtesy of International with Monument,
New York

Léger, 1986
Acrylic on canvas, 48 × 48 ″
Collection of Collins and Milazzo, New York

Mondo Cane, 1986
Acrylic on canvas, 36 × 36 ″
Collection of Corrado Levi, Milan

DAVID ROBBINS
Born in 1957. Lives in New York City.

Books Encased in Lucite, 1986
Four paperbacks in lucite, lifesize
Courtesy of 303 Gallery, New York

Demographics, 1984-87
Three color photographs with silkscreen and
glass, 40 × 30 ″ or 30 × 20 ″
Courtesy of 303 Gallery and Nature Morte,
New York

JOHN SCARLETT-DAVIS
Born in 1957. Lives in New York City.

* *A Trip Through the Wardrobes of the Mind*, 1983
Color video, 5 minutes
Courtesy of Electronic Arts Intermix, New
York, and London Video Arts

ANDRES SERRANO
Born in 1950. Lives in New York City.

Dread, 1987

* *Gold Christ*, 1987

Yellow River, 1987

Color photographs, each: 40 × 60″ or 60 × 40″
Courtesy of Stux Gallery, New York

SHELLY SILVER
Born in 1957. Lives in New York City.

* *Meet the People*, 1986
Color video, 15 minutes
Courtesy of the artist

MICHAEL SMITH
Born in 1951. Lives in New York City.

MIKE, 1987
Color video, 2 minutes 45 seconds
Courtesy of Electronic Arts Intermix, New York

SARAH TUFT
Born in 1957. Lives in New York City.

* *Don't Make Me Up*, 1986
Color video, 3 minutes 43 seconds
Courtesy of the artist

Staff

Kimball Augustus
Security

Lauren Berry
Development Assistant

Gayle Brandel
Administrator

Helen Carr
Special Events Coordinator

Mary Clancy
Assistant to the Director

Russell Ferguson
Librarian

Karen Fiss
Curatorial Assistant

Rod Goodrow
Assistant, Director's Office

Lynn Gumpert
Senior Curator

Elon Joseph
Security

Margo Machida
Planning and Development

Phil Mariani
Publications Coordinator

Portland McCormick
Curatorial Secretary

Eric Miles
High School Program

James Minden
Operations Manager

John Neely
Head of Education

Jill L. Newmark
Registrar

Barbara Niblock
Bookkeeper

William Olander
Curator

Sara Palmer
Public Affairs Assistant

Wayne Rottman
Security/Operations

Aleya Saad
Admissions Coordinator

Larry Saul
Youth Program

Cindy Smith
Preparator/Assistant to the Registrar

Virginia Strull
Director of Planning and Development

Terrie Sultan
Director of Public Affairs

Neville Thompson
Assistant to Operations Manager

Robbin Tolan
Receptionist

Marcia Tucker
Director

Brian Wallis
Adjunct Editor

Suzanna Watkins
Assistant to the Administrator

Margaret Weissbach
Coordinator of Docents and Interns

Board of Trustees

Jay Chiat

Gregory C. Clark

Maureen Cogan

Elaine Dannheisser

Richard Ekstract

John Fitting, Jr.

Arthur A. Goldberg
Treasurer

Allen Goldring

Eugene Paul Gorman

Paul C. Harper, Jr.

Sharon K. Hoge

Martin E. Kantor

Nanette Laitman

Vera G. List
Vice-President

Henry Luce III
President

Mary McFadden

Therese M. Molloy

Patrick Savin

Paul T. Schnell

Herman Schwartzman

Laura Skoler

Marcia Tucker